Draw more things for the bears.

• Uses language of comparison, bigger/smaller than.

Notes/date:

3.4

③

I found out

I found out

• Can estimate holds more/less than.   Notes/date:

• Can use non-standard measures.

$$4 + 1 =$$

$$4 + 2 =$$

$$\square + \square = \square$$

$$\square + \square = \square$$

$$\square + \square = \square$$

$$\square + \square = \square$$

- Can add with small numbers.   Notes/date:
- Recognises and can use language for + and =.

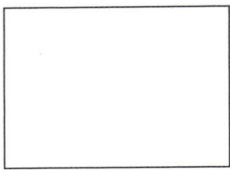

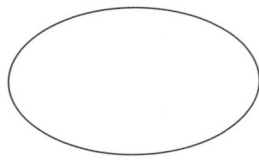

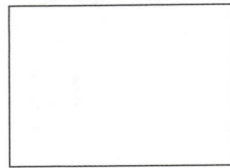

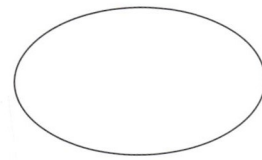

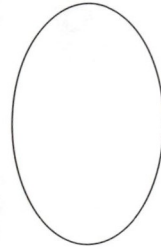

$$4 - 1 = $$

$$4 - 2 = $$

$$\square \quad \square \quad \square \quad = \quad \square$$

$$\square \quad \square \quad \square \quad = \quad \square$$

$$\square \quad \square \quad \square \quad = \quad \square$$

$$\square \quad \square \quad \square \quad = \quad \square$$

- Can use ⊟ key appropriately.   Notes/date:
- Can use the words 'take away', etc appropriately.

6   3.5

· · · · · 5

3 and 2 is 5

3 + 2 = 5

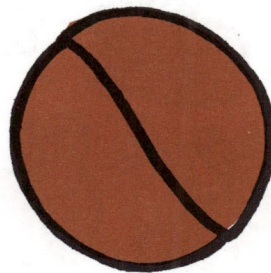

☐ and ☐ is ☐

☐ + ☐ = ☐

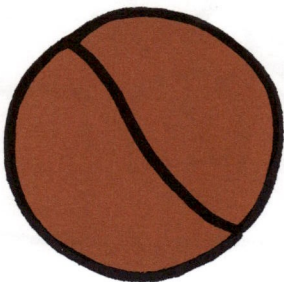

☐ and ☐ is ☐

☐ and ☐ is ☐

- Understands conservation of number.   Notes/date:
- Can add two numbers.

3.6   ⑦

Draw 7

Draw 10.

ten IO IO IO

- Can count to 10.   Notes/date:
- Can check totals.

I measured with

I found out

I measured with

I found out

Make patterns with 4 squares.
They must touch.
How many?

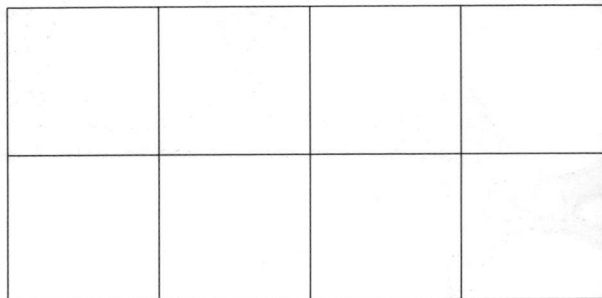

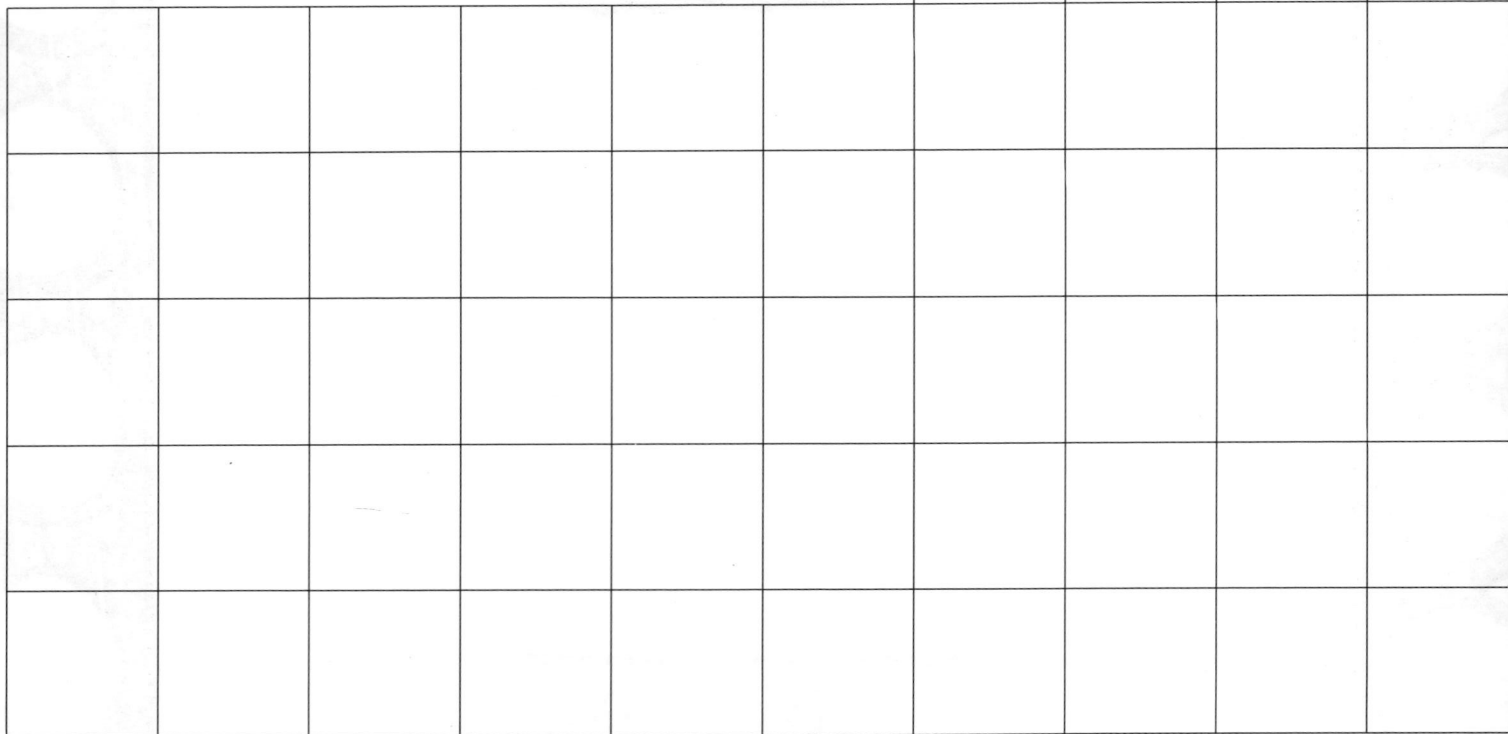

Now use triangles.
How many?

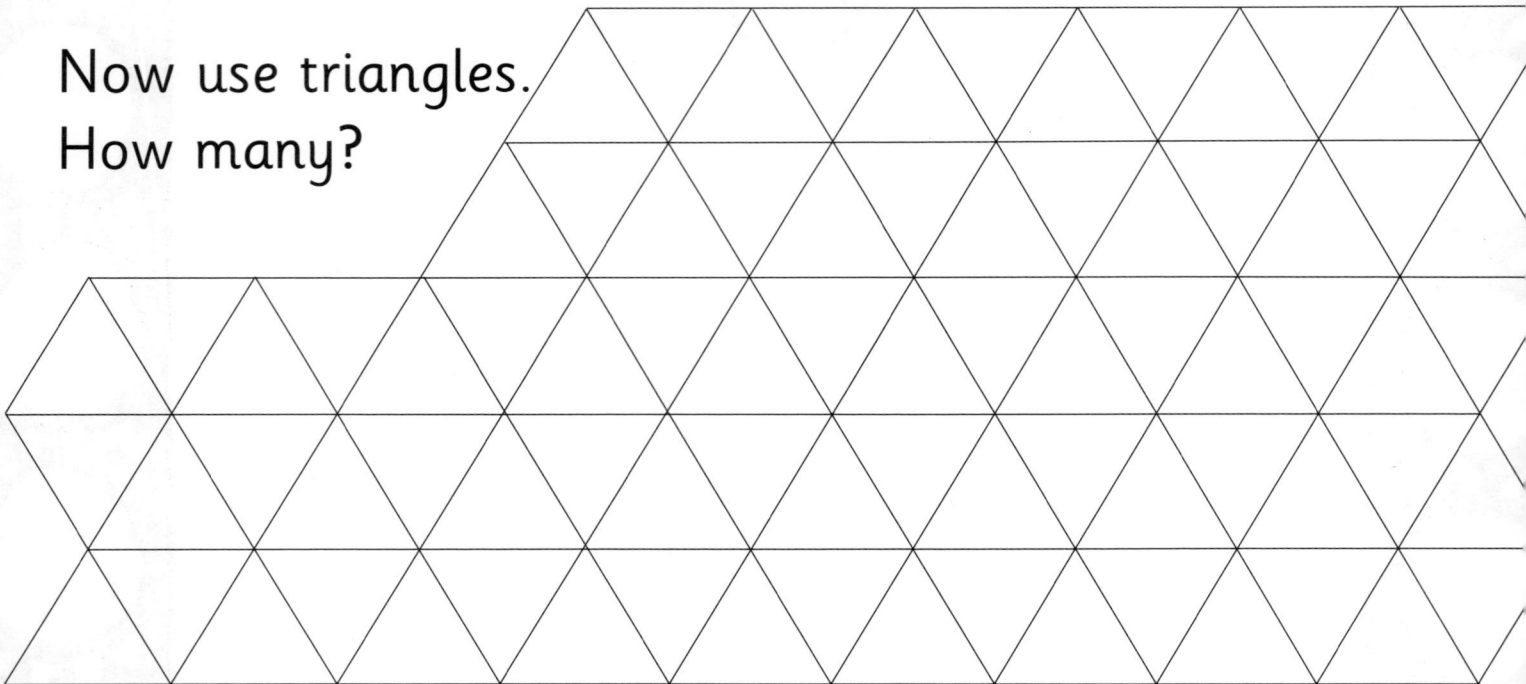

• Can make a simple pattern.   Notes/date:
• Can talk about shapes.

You need

 cup    jug

How many  in

Colour

You need

 cup    funnel    wide bottle    thin bottle

Estimate		cupfuls
	wide bottle	
	thin bottle	

Count		cupfuls
	wide bottle	
	thin bottle	

Which bottle holds most?

• Can estimate capacity.   Notes/date:

• Can count cupfuls.

Ask friends which drink they like best.
Draw the drinks on the graph.

6					
5					
4					
3					
2					
1					
	water	milk	orange	lemon	coke

• Can collect and record data.   Notes/date:
• Can interpret data.

12   3.7

Give Ted five buttons

pockets

balloons

3

five

2

one

six

Write ways to make 5.

= 5

= 5

= 5

1

5

Join.

This is good for building.

This is good for rolling.

This slides.

Make a model with bricks.
Count.

• Can sort and classify sets of objects.   Notes/date:
• Uses attributes of shapes when
  building models.